SERVICE IN THE
ARMED FORCES

BY DUCHESS HARRIS, JD, PHD

WITH JILL C. WHEELER

CONTENT CONSULTANT

HEATH FOGG DAVIS, PHD
DIRECTOR, GENDER, SEXUALITY,
AND WOMEN'S STUDIES PROGRAM
TEMPLE UNIVERSITY

BEING
LGBTQ
IN AMERICA

Essential Library

An Imprint of Abdo Publishing | abdobooks.com

ABDOBOOKS.COM

Published by Abdo Publishing, a division of ABDO, PO Box 398166, Minneapolis, Minnesota 55439. Copyright © 2020 by Abdo Consulting Group, Inc. International copyrights reserved in all countries. No part of this book may be reproduced in any form without written permission from the publisher. Essential Library™ is a trademark and logo of Abdo Publishing.

Printed in the United States of America, North Mankato, Minnesota.
042019
092019

THIS BOOK CONTAINS
RECYCLED MATERIALS

Cover Photo: Shutterstock Images
Interior Photos: Senior Airman Matthew Lotz/US Air Force, 5; Shutterstock Images, 9; Janson George/Shutterstock Images, 12; Light Field Studios/Shutterstock Images, 14; Yana Paskova/Washington Post/Getty Images, 17; North Wind Picture Archives, 19, 21; National Photo Company Collection/Library of Congress, 23; Bettmann/Getty Images, 27; Library of Congress, 28; Everett Historical/Shutterstock Images, 31, 38; George Karger/Pix Inc./The Life Images Collection/Getty Images, 33; Fox Photos/ Hulton Archive/Getty Images, 35; dpa/Picture Alliance/dpa/AP Images, 43; Louis Liotta/New York Post Archives/NYP Holdings/The New York Post/Getty Images, 47; Michael Schwartz/New York Post Archives/NYP Holdings/The New York Post/Getty Images, 49; Patsy Lynch/Alamy Live News/Alamy, 52; Fred W. McDarrah/Premium Archive/Getty Images, 55; Justin Sutcliffe/AP Images, 57; Mark Peterson/Corbis/ Corbis Historical/Getty Images, 62; Showtime Networks/Photofest, 66; Moshe Bursuker/AP Images, 69; Alex Wong/Getty Images News/Getty Images, 71; Charles Dharapak/AP Images, 75; Craig F. Walker/The Denver Post/Getty Images, 76; Staff Sgt. Vern Dubois Jr./US Army, 79; Lance Cpl. Matthew Myers/US Marines, 83; Lance Cpl. Mark Fike/US Marines, 85; Senior Airman Ashley Nicole Taylor/US Air Force, 87; Mandel Ngan/AFP/Getty Images, 93; Wave Break Media/Shutterstock Images, 98

Editor: Megan Ellis
Designer: Melissa Martin

LIBRARY OF CONGRESS CONTROL NUMBER: 2018966016

PUBLISHER'S CATALOGING-IN-PUBLICATION DATA

Names: Harris, Duchess, author. | Wheeler, Jill C., author.
Title: LGBTQ service in the armed forces / by Duchess Harris and Jill C. Wheeler.
Description: Minneapolis, Minnesota : Abdo Publishing, 2020 | Series: Being LGBTQ in America | Includes online resources and index.
Identifiers: ISBN 9781532119071 (lib. bdg.) | ISBN 9781532173257 (ebook)
Subjects: LCSH: LGBTQ people--Juvenile literature. | Minorities in the military- -Juvenile literature. | Sexual minority veterans--Juvenile literature. | Discrimination in the military--Juvenile literature.
Classification: DDC 355.0086--dc23

CONTENTS

Eric Fanning served as the secretary of the army from May 18, 2016 to January 20, 2017.

NEW
ADMINISTRATION

O n May 18, 2016, President Barack Obama appointed Eric Fanning the twenty-second secretary of the army. Fanning thus became the first openly gay leader of a US military service and the highest-ranking openly gay Pentagon official in US history. Prior to accepting the job, he served as acting undersecretary of the army, undersecretary of the air force, and deputy secretary of the navy. Fanning resigned from the post at the end of the Obama administration and took a job in private industry.

During Obama's presidency, LGBTQ servicepeople began to serve openly in the military. But with the change of a presidential administration, the nation got new rules. In the early morning of July 26, 2017, President Donald Trump used his Twitter account to issue a new directive. It read, "After consultation with my Generals and military experts, please be advised that the United States Government will not accept or

allow transgender individuals to serve in any capacity in the U.S. Military."[1] In subsequent tweets, President Trump indicated that the decision was based on the large medical costs created by allowing transgender (trans) people to serve in the military. A transgender person is someone whose gender identity is different from the sex they were assigned at birth.

Historically, the military's medical code excluded trans people from serving or led to their discharge. It excluded anyone who had a diagnosis of a psychosexual disorder, or a mental disorder related to sex or sexuality. At previous points in history, cross-dressing and being trans were considered psychosexual disorders. However, in 2016 President Obama's administration enacted a policy that stated that trans people

AN UNCERTAIN FUTURE FOR TRANSGENDER SOLDIERS

People serving in the military who have undergone or who will undergo gender-affirming surgery face an uncertain future as of 2018. One such person is Specialist Alex Ketchum, a 22-year-old infantry member. She started her transition in late 2015, eight months prior to the lifting of the ban on trans service people. In the following months, she completed her physical transition and began changing her gender in the military's personnel system. Ketchum became one of the first women to serve in the US infantry.

After the ban on transgender soldiers was announced, Ketchum is hoping for good news about her continued military service, but she's also preparing for bad news. According to Ketchum, even if she is discharged for her gender identity, she does not regret serving in the military.

could serve openly in the US military. But in 2017, Trump's policy reversed the decision from the previous year. Some federal judges placed injunctions on the ban in 2018. This meant that the ban would not take effect while judges decided the legality of the ban. However, in January 2019, the US Supreme Court ruled that the ban could remain in place while civil cases about the ban made their way through the federal court system. Trans people were then barred from enlisting, and openly trans servicepeople were at risk of receiving less than honorable discharges because of their gender identity.

For many advocates in the lesbian, gay, bisexual, transgender, and queer (LGBTQ) community, the ban on trans soldiers sounded all too familiar. Many of the arguments were similar to those made in favor of a previous ban on gay and lesbian soldiers known as Don't Ask, Don't Tell (DADT). Some proponents of the ban argued that trans soldiers harmed national security. They argued that trans people were likely to suffer from mental illness, which would reduce the effectiveness of the military. A report from the US Department of Defense (DOD) noted that scientists did not know how effective medical care was for people whose birth gender and gender identity were different. That condition, known as gender dysphoria, is a psychological condition in which a person feels distress because of the sex they were assigned at birth. The DOD report stated that soldiers with gender dysphoria were medically unfit for deployment. For many LGBTQ advocates, the ban felt like a dramatic reversal of a hard-won trend toward more acceptance of LGBTQ soldiers.

OPPOSING FORCES

LGBTQ people have always been a part of human societies and thus a part of the militaries used to defend those societies.

However, the presence of LGBTQ service members often has been viewed as a threat to the military tradition itself.

Some people perceive the military as more manly than other career choices. To them, the military turns strong boys into even more masculine men. This image weakens when other groups of people who are perceived as less manly, such as women and LGBTQ soldiers, join the military.

TRANS PIONEER CHRISTINE JORGENSEN

In late 1952, the *New York Daily News* reported that a former army soldier had traveled to Denmark for gender-affirming surgery. Christine Jorgensen was a World War II (1939–1945) veteran who became inspired by more-accepting views of gender and sexuality in Europe.

The *New York Daily News* story quickly became one of the most popular of the year. Jorgensen, a photographer and actress, took advantage of the media buzz to educate the public about the differences between sexuality and gender identity. Her work led to a better understanding of gender identity in the United States. Her bravery gave new hope to other trans people who were experiencing similar feelings.

Starting in 2016, women could serve in combat roles in the US military.

For example, Brigadier General Elizabeth Hoisington of the Women's Auxiliary Army Corps (WAAC), who had never served in a combat role, argued in 1978 that women should not be allowed to serve in combat roles "because the average woman is simply not physically, mentally and emotionally qualified to

EXPERTS WEIGH IN ON BANNING TRANSGENDER TROOPS

In the spring of 2018, six former surgeons general signed a statement disputing the DOD's claims in regard to the medical fitness of trans troops. The surgeon general is the primary spokesperson for topics related to the health of the population as a whole. The surgeons general stated that they felt trans troops were as medically fit as their cisgender (cis) peers. A cisgender person is someone whose gender identity matches the sex they were assigned at birth. The surgeons general added that in their opinion, there was no medically valid reason to exclude transgender troops from military service or limit their access to medically necessary care. The surgeons general stated that there was a global medical consensus that trans medical care is reliable, safe, and effective.

perform well in a combat situation for extended periods." She added, "It's pretty plain that God intended women to bear the children and men to be the protectors in our society."[2]

The military defends the nation. For the entirety of US military history, LGBTQ soldiers have been the targets of discrimination, prejudice, hatred, and violence from other soldiers. These harmful behaviors by non-LGBTQ soldiers reflected similar actions against LGBTQ people in civil society. However, military and political leaders justified these actions by pointing to two key military beliefs. The first argument states that cohesion cannot happen when the group members are diverse. The second is that unit cohesion leads to a more effective military. However, both of these arguments have been debunked by research.

WAR OF WORDS AND DATA

Advocates for LGBTQ people in the military say that LGBTQ soldiers minimally impact the military's budget. In response to the ban on trans soldiers, these advocates cited a 2016 report from the RAND Corporation. The report found that allowing trans people to serve in the military would have minimal impact on readiness and health-care costs. The report also estimated health-care costs would increase by between 0.04 and 0.13 percent if trans people were allowed in active duty. In addition, the report indicated that less than one-tenth of 1 percent of the total military force would seek medical care related to gender transition that might impact their ability to do their job.[3]

Advocates also argued that trans soldiers are not medically unfit for active duty. The RAND study noted that in 2016–2017, 393 of the 994 service members diagnosed with gender dysphoria deployed to Iraq and Afghanistan. Only one of those soldiers returned early due to mental health reasons.[4]

The ban on trans soldiers called attention to the LGBTQ community's desire for an equal opportunity to serve its country. A 2013 Harvard Kennedy School report stated that approximately 20 percent of trans people were serving or had served in the military.[5] That is almost double the percentage of the total US population's military service, though researchers

Some LGBTQ soldiers and activists march in Pride parades around the United States.

are unsure why. In addition, the DOD reported that only 9,000 service members had identified as trans since they were allowed to do so during the Obama administration. That number is a small segment of the total military force of 1.3 million active duty members.[6]

The ban on trans soldiers created new discussions among people who had been unaware that trans people could not serve in the military. For LGBTQ activists, the ban was just the latest in a string of actions that have forced LGBTQ people to silently endure discrimination, humiliation, and even violence if they wish to serve their country.

TWITTER HASHTAGS

President Trump used Twitter to announce his ban on transgender troops. Not surprisingly, the social media platform has become a place for supporters of trans troops to express themselves as well. One of the ways people have opposed the ban is by using the hashtag #TransBanTweetUp. LGBTQ advocacy groups, including the Human Rights Campaign and Lambda Legal, encouraged opponents of the ban to use the hashtag again in July 2018 to mark the anniversary of the initial ban.

MILITARY AND SOCIAL POLICY

There are many reasons why someone may want to join the military. They may feel passionate about defending the United States. They may be interested in higher education or better

Some people join the military because they have family members who served in the military.

job opportunities than would be available to them as a civilian. They may have family members who served in the military.

The military has long been at the forefront of successfully integrating marginalized or excluded groups into US society, whether those groups were people of color, women, or the LGBTQ community. For example, the US military racially integrated all units in 1948. This meant that white soldiers and African American soldiers could serve in the same military units.

In contrast, the United States did not outlaw employment discrimination based on race, color, religion, sex, or national origin until the Civil Rights Act of 1964.

Each time the military took steps forward in terms of equality, it faced many critics and a challenging road toward understanding and acceptance. But no integration of troops, whether gay and straight, or cisgender and transgender, has decreased the military's effectiveness. The military's success in and dedication to upholding the right to serve will continue to be a powerful force for social change.

DISCUSSION STARTERS

- Why might trans people wish to serve in the military even when they know they may face discrimination?
- Why might people believe that LGBTQ soldiers would harm the military?
- How might a military unit that includes LGBTQ soldiers be more effective than one that does not include LGBTQ soldiers?

MILITARY DISCHARGES

Military service members do not quit their jobs in the same way people do in civilian life. Service members must obtain a discharge in order to be released from their service. There are several different kinds of military discharges. The type of discharge a service member receives can make a huge difference in the life of that service member, as well as in the lives of any family members.

The preferred discharge is an honorable discharge. It indicates a service member received a good or excellent rating for their service time. Service members receiving an honorable discharge qualify for all veterans' benefits, including health care, education credits, and insurance. Lesser levels of discharge include a general or administrative discharge, an undesirable discharge, and a dishonorable discharge. These discharges indicate the service member failed to live up to all codes of military conduct. Any of these discharges is regarded as shameful in both the military community and civil society. These types of discharges also entail a loss of some or all veterans' benefits.

LGBTQ service members who were discharged for their sexual orientation did not receive honorable discharges. In World War II, US military policy directed that gay soldiers should be committed to a military hospital, examined, and summarily discharged under what was called a section 8 regulation. These soldiers were given a less than honorable discharge called a blue discharge, which was often referred to as a blue ticket.

A 1970s study examined the impact of less than honorable discharges on LGBTQ personnel. The study showed 39 percent received general discharges, 55 percent received undesirable discharges, and 6 percent received dishonorable discharges. More than 80 percent of veterans did not fight these decisions, due in large part to shame.[7]

Landon Wilson was discharged from the US Navy in 2014 for being a trans man.

SHE MAY NOT ALWAYS
FIGHT FOR ME

George Washington was the
commander in chief of
the Continental Army.

LGBTQ SOLDIERS
IN THE 1700s AND 1800s

Discrimination against LGBTQ people in the military began even before there was officially a US military. In March 1778, Lieutenant Frederick Gotthold Enslin was the first recorded person to be expelled from a military unit in the United States due to his sexual orientation. Enslin had enlisted in the Continental Army in 1777. The Continental Army was the loose confederation of soldiers assembled from the 13 colonies that were to become the United States of America.

Records of Enslin indicate he was educated and financially secure. However, military court records indicate Enslin was discovered with another soldier in his cabin. He was subsequently court-martialed and found guilty of sodomy and perjury. The court at the Valley Forge base sentenced Enslin to

TWO-SPIRIT SOLDIERS

Many Native American nations traditionally recognized more than two genders. In the 1990s, Native American activists coined the term *two-spirit* to refer to people outside the gender binary across many different Native American tribes.[1] Most two-spirit people encountered by white traders, explorers, and missionaries were people who had the bodily appearance of men but performed tasks traditionally associated with women. The Cheyenne nation also had two-spirit people who had the bodily appearance of women but who dressed as men and participated in hunting and war parties.

Osh-Tisch was a two-spirit person in the Crow nation. She helped other Native Americans defeat US Army forces in the Battle of the Rosebud in 1876. Osh-Tisch, whose name translates to "finds them and kills them," was known both for her ferocity in battle and for her sewing skills.[2] Because of this, she was seen as having traits of both masculine and feminine people.

As Western religions, missionaries, government agents, soldiers, and settlers attacked and interfered with tribal communities, many tribes lost their traditions. In particular, two-spirit people were condemned and sometimes attacked. As a result, two-spirit traditions and practices went underground or disappeared in many tribes.

be dismissed with infamy. In the tradition of the time, Enslin was literally drummed out of the Continental Army. He was forced to walk away as the fife and drum corps played and the other soldiers looked on.

Ironically, Enslin's departure came at the same time that the Continental Army was receiving much-needed training at the hands of a decorated military officer who was also gay. Baron Friedrich von Steuben was a Prussian military professional and strategist. He had whipped his countrymen into the strongest military power in Europe. George Washington hired Steuben in early 1778 to reshape the US military, which lacked

Some of his colleagues and superiors may have known that Baron von Steuben had relationships with other men.

BEFORE THE TERM LGBTQ

The first known use of the term *homosexual* in the English language dates back to 1892.[3] Yet passionate same-sex friendships were common among both men and women in the 1800s. Actions that today might be viewed as those reserved for people in the LGBTQ community, such as two men sharing the same bed, were at that time considered a natural part of heterosexuality. Many educated women of means also enjoyed ambiguous female partnerships called "Boston marriages." The thinking at the time was that women were nonsexual to begin with, so if they had no husbands, they would have no interest in sex.

discipline and supplies. It also suffered from low morale.

Von Steuben became the inspector general for Washington's weary troops. He taught the soldiers better ways to fight and drilled them until their discipline improved. Eventually, von Steuben became Washington's chief of staff and wrote a drill manual, parts of which were still in use as of 2018. Many historians believe his work was instrumental in helping the colonies win the Revolutionary War (1775–1783).

SIGN OF THE TIMES

Some historians believe von Steuben's contemporaries knew about his sexuality. However, von Steuben's abilities as a military leader allowed him to remain in the army. Von Steuben's case was helped by the culture of the time as well. Though sodomy was officially a criminal offense in the

Commodore Stephen Decatur, *pictured*, had an intense friendship with Richard Somers.

American colonies, intense friendships among men were widely accepted. Von Steuben's aides, Alexander Hamilton and John Laurens, maintained such a friendship with seemingly no repercussions. The terms *homosexual* and *heterosexual* did not enter the US lexicon until the early 1900s.[4]

This cloak of friendship also likely shielded the relationship of two early naval heroes, Stephen Decatur and Richard Somers. They had been friends since they were children. The two were commissioned together in 1798 as a part of the new US Navy. Decatur and Somers became captains in the navy at a very young age. Shortly after, a mysterious explosion during a mission killed Somers. While Decatur had a distinguished naval career and rose to the rank of commodore, he never truly recovered from the loss of Somers. To the end of his life, he wore a gold ring that Somers had given him just before taking off on his final, ill-fated mission.

LGBTQ PEOPLE IN THE CIVIL WAR

Gay and lesbian people responded when the nation called for service members during the American Civil War (1861–1865). In his letters, renowned poet Walt Whitman indicated he was involved with several gay Union soldiers during the conflict. Additionally, Union general Philip Sheridan recorded an instance when two lesbian soldiers, disguised as men, were discovered after drinking too much and nearly drowning.

Gay and lesbian military personnel make an appearance in Confederate historical records as well. Confederate major general Patrick Cleburne was famous for his daring attacks on enemy lines. A native of Ireland, Cleburne had gained critical military experience with the British Army before moving to the United States. He was in a two-year relationship with Captain Irving Buck, which his colleagues knew about. Cleburne died in battle in 1864.

Following the Civil War, many service members headed west to fight in armed conflicts against Native Americans. One story from that era concerns someone named Mrs. Nash who married a succession of soldiers at various western forts in the late 1860s and 1870s. As soon as one of Mrs. Nash's husbands left the army, she would marry someone else. Mrs. Nash was married to a member of General George Custer's Seventh Cavalry when she passed away. Her husband was away on a campaign. Fellow army wives were preparing Mrs. Nash's body for burial when they discovered that Mrs. Nash appeared to have male genitals.

EXHIBIT HONORS TRANSGENDER CIVIL WAR HEROES

In November 2014, photo media artist and professor Scott Angus held an exhibit in Saint Louis, Missouri. It told the story of women who lived, dressed, and fought as men in the American Civil War. Angus had discovered portraits of these female soldiers. He reworked eight of the images with colors from the trans flag—light pink, white, and light blue—to highlight the past while bridging it to the future. Angus chose soldiers who would likely be considered part of the LGBTQ community today. The exhibit celebrated the sacrifice and bravery of these LGBTQ pioneers in early US history.

EARLY TRANSGENDER SERVICE MEMBERS

There were also people who may have been transgender who enlisted during the Civil War. Albert Cashier joined the Illinois Infantry Regiment. He fought in many battles in the war but missed out on an army pension because he refused to take a required physical. When Cashier was injured in a 1911 car accident, doctors discovered that he had the bodily appearance of a woman. Cashier was committed to an insane asylum after the discovery. However, his fellow veterans made sure that Cashier was buried with full military honors when he died in 1915.

By some estimates, at least 250 Civil War soldiers were women who dressed as men.[5] As the war went on and recruiters became ever more desperate for anyone who could carry a gun, it was even easier for women to enlist as men. It is impossible to say definitively that these soldiers were trans. They may have been cisgender people who wanted to join the army but were unable because of their sex. According to Elizabeth Leonard, a history professor at Colby College, people at the time "wouldn't know what in the world you

THE EVOLUTION OF SEX AND GENDER

The word *gender* was used for centuries to describe the quality of being male or female. Likewise, *sex* historically has been used to refer to the biological elements of male and female as they are assigned at birth. Both of these elements contributed to the social norms that determined in- and out-group status as related to gender identification and sexual activity.

The concept of gender as a societal representation of male and female first appeared in the mid-1940s. This ushered in the concept of gender as a social construction, separate from the biology of sex.

KADY BROWNELL
IN ARMY COSTUME.

Eng.d by G.E.Perine AC.t N.Y.

During the Civil War, some women, such as Kady
Brownell, fought alongside male Union soldiers.

US Army medical officer Mary Edwards Walker preferred dressing in men's clothing.

meant by the [word] transgender, but there have [been] women serving in men's dress in armies since the beginning of wars."[6]

Dr. Mary Edwards Walker was the only woman surgeon for the Union Army. She became known as the "Little Lady in Pants." Walker never claimed to be a man, but she dressed in men's fashion, such as in top hats and tails. Walker's distinguished career included her arrest as a spy when she was caught treating wounded soldiers behind enemy lines. However, her fashion choices were controversial. According to Leonard, "People [celebrated] the courage of the women who cut their hair and passed as men. But they had no idea what to do with Mary Walker. She really was the precursor for the idea of 'I am just going to be who I am.'"[7]

DISCUSSION STARTERS

- Why do you think soldiers in the Continental Army treated von Steuben and Enslin differently?

- Do you think that all of the women who dressed as men in the Union Army were in the LGBTQ community? Why or why not?

- How are some of the clothing "rules" for different genders still used today?

During World War I and World War II, LGBTQ soldiers had to remain hidden while serving.

LGBTQ SOLDIERS IN
THE WORLD WARS

M ilitary law in the United States codified homosexuality as a crime during World War I (1914–1918). The United States entered the conflict in 1917. This was also when the Articles of War of 1916 went into effect. The 1916 revision of these articles criminalized assault with intent to commit sodomy. In 1920, the articles were revised to criminalize sodomy itself, whether the act was consensual or assault. These changes to military law led to the imprisonment of many gay sailors and soldiers in the 1920s and 1930s.

During World War I, people began to think that soldiers should be not only punished for homosexuality but also not allowed to join the military at all. This era also saw the beginning of investigation into the medical model of homosexuality. In 1918, San Francisco doctor Albert Abrams wrote that "from a military viewpoint, the homosexualist is not

DRAG IN THE MILITARY

During World War I, drag shows were kept secret and happened away from military bases at places like the YMCA. But beginning in World War II, drag shows were officially sanctioned by the military. They were for troop entertainment. Additionally, they helped gay service members connect with one another. Shows such as Irving Berlin's *This Is the Army* featured female impersonators. This offered a welcome break from the closeted, or hidden, life that many LGBTQ service members were forced to lead to avoid a discharge.

World War II allowed many heterosexual and questioning service members to experience sexual freedom and experimentation far from family and community. Interviews with soldiers also indicate that most gay soldiers were accepted by their peers. A shipment of dresses for a drag show might be embraced by gay and straight soldiers alike simply for the camaraderie and entertainment it offered.

only [dangerous], but an ineffective fighter."[1] Abrams also invented a device he claimed could detect homosexual military recruits by measuring radiation levels around their testicles. Abrams's work was later debunked, but the damage in public society had already been done. The military stepped up efforts to find and remove gay service members.

Sailor Ervin Arnold was recovering in a naval hospital in early 1919 when he heard a fellow sailor speak of drag shows, dances, and more at the army and navy Young Men's Christian Association (YMCA). Arnold informed his superiors of what he had learned, and the navy assigned Arnold to lead a sting operation involving the Newport, Rhode Island, YMCA.

US soldiers performed in drag for plays such as Irving Berlin's *This Is the Army.*

Arnold recruited 13 enlistees to act as undercover agents. They were instructed to participate in all activities that took place there and report back. Within months, 15 sailors had been arrested for "lack of moral perspective."[2] They were then court-martialed and sent to military prison. Arnold and the officials who approved his plan were later censured by a US Senate subcommittee because Arnold used enlisted men to entrap the suspected gay sailors. The legal term *entrapment* refers to the government creating a scenario to trick people into committing illegal acts.

START OF THE
GAY RIGHTS MOVEMENT

The Scientific Humanitarian Committee (SHC) was founded in Berlin, Germany, in 1897. It was the world's leading emancipation group for gay people at the time. The SHC was dedicated to overturning the provision of the German Criminal Code that made sex acts between two men a crime. The work of the SHC inspired another German man, Henry Gerber. He had immigrated to the United States and served in the US Army in World War I. Henry Gerber founded the Society for Human Rights (SHR), which was the first documented gay rights organization in the United States. The SHR, the SHC, and others began spreading the idea that gay people should be recognized for their contributions to society. The groups

ALLEN IRVIN BERNSTEIN

After trying to pick up another soldier in 1944, army staff sergeant Allen Irvin Bernstein received a blue ticket, or a less than honorable discharge for homosexual activity. He was arrested by military police and sent to a psychiatric ward at Camp Lee, Virginia. Then he was discharged. He appealed his discharge and sent the court a 140-page document defending homosexuality. Bernstein's paper, *Millions of Queers (Our Homo America)*, was ignored and forgotten until a researcher at the National Library of Medicine found it in 2010. Bernstein was denied veterans' benefits due to his blue discharge. He continued to file appeals until 1981, when the army retroactively converted his blue discharge into an honorable discharge.

began advocating not only for an end to sodomy laws but also for the right to serve openly in the military.

World War I also created the material for a groundbreaking development in LGBTQ literature. *The Well of Loneliness* by Radclyffe Hall, a lesbian author, was published in 1928. The novel is the story of an Englishwoman named Stephen who drives an ambulance on the western front in World War I. She falls in love with another ambulance driver, Mary. Almost immediately, a British court banned the book, declaring it obscene due to its promotion of "unnatural practices

Radclyffe Hall, *right*, published eight novels, but only *The Well of Loneliness* had lesbian themes.

between women."[3] *The Well of Loneliness* is considered by many to be the first major lesbian novel.

FROM CRIME TO ILLNESS

Though psychiatrists had warned against allowing lesbian and gay soldiers to enlist in the military since World War I, a formal US military policy did not exist until 1942. That year, military psychiatrists created guides that they believed would allow US military recruiters to spot and eliminate LGBTQ recruits. These guides were first used in the months before the United States entered World War II (1939–1945). At that point, the military faced a task of enlisting 16 million soldiers for the war effort. But homosexuality, as it was called at the time, was seen as an illness. Gay men and lesbians were considered psychologically unfit for service. By that time, more people were inclined to treat homosexuality as a mental illness instead of a crime.

Approximately 18 million US men went in front of World War II draft boards and medical inspectors before entering the military. Only approximately 5,000 men were screened out based on the guides developed to identify homosexuality.[4] Some people were discovered and discharged later. Yet by the end of the war, thousands of LGBTQ people had served in all branches of the military. Some saw enlisting as an opportunity to meet other LGBTQ people. Some enlisted without understanding their gender identity or sexual orientation.

HITLER'S PERSECUTION OF LGBTQ PEOPLE

Germany's Nazi Party under Adolf Hitler persecuted homosexual men during its years in power. Approximately 50,000 men were convicted for homosexuality during the Nazi regime. Between 5,000 and 15,000 of them were interned in concentration camps, where up to 60 percent of them died.[7] "Asocial" women, which included lesbians, feminists, and sex workers, were also convicted and sent to concentration camps. Gay men were forced to wear a pink triangle on their clothes, while asocial women were forced to wear a black triangle.

When Allied forces liberated concentration camps in 1945, homosexuality was still a criminal offense. Many of these men were transferred to other prisons in Germany to complete their sentences. Homosexuality was not decriminalized in Germany until 1969. This was due in large part to a string of conservative governments that supported platforms of family values and traditional morals.

Most simply wanted to serve their country. As one gay veteran said, "We were not about to be deprived of the privilege of serving our country in a time of great national emergency by virtue of some stupid regulation about being gay."[5]

Gay service members had to avoid detection in order to stay in the military. Due to their secrecy, as well as the military's overwhelming need for their services, fewer than one-half of 1 percent of World War II soldiers were discharged for homosexuality.[6] This is because superiors were more likely to ignore soldiers' sexuality because they needed all the soldiers they could get. Additionally, many gay and lesbian people from small towns or rural parts of the country found the military more freeing. Because superior officers ignored sexuality

THIS IS MY WAR TOO!
WOMEN'S ARMY AUXILIARY CORPS
UNITED · STATES · ARMY

Though women could not serve in the US military, organizations such as the WAAC allowed them to participate in the war effort.

during wartime, these soldiers received less scrutiny than they did back home.

Auxiliary military service organizations such as the WAAC enabled women to get involved in the war effort during World War II. Despite an effort to present its members as sexually moral, the WAAC suffered multiple slander campaigns. These campaigns accused WAAC members of lesbianism, promiscuity, and prostitution. In an effort to maintain its image in the public eye, the WAAC prohibited nonheterosexual members. However, organizations such as WAAC enabled women in the LGBTQ community to explore their gender and sexuality by covertly allowing them to meet other people in the community. If they were silent about their sexuality, most of society allowed them equal status because they were helping with the war effort.

ROSIE THE LGBTQ RIVETER

In March 2014, the Rosie the Riveter World War II Home Front National Park in Richmond, California, made an announcement. It called for submissions of stories of LGBTQ civilians who contributed to the war effort for inclusion in a 2015 traveling exhibit. The initiative was part of a larger trend within the US government to recognize LGBTQ people for their contributions throughout US history.

The first story submitted was about Bev Hickok. Hickok, a lesbian, worked on the assembly line at the Douglas Aircraft Company factory. She recalls a warm welcome from fellow lesbian workers on her very first day. "Evidently they took one look at me and said, 'There's another one,'" Hickok recalled.[8]

KEEPING IT QUIET

Despite military regulations during this time, most LGBTQ service members carried out their duties and quietly avoided prison. Some LGBTQ service members were simply transferred to other roles where their personal lives would be under less scrutiny. According to WAAC sergeant Johnnie Phelps, "I found there was a tolerance for lesbianism if they needed you. If you had a job . . . where bodies were needed, they tolerated anything, just about."[9]

RACE, SEXUALITY, AND SODOMY

A Civil War–era legal guide said that white men detained for sodomy should be subjected to an examination but black men detained for sodomy should be subjected to trial. Army discharges for homosexuality in World War II continued this discrimination. The typical discharge for people accused of homosexuality was a blue discharge. More than 22 percent of all blue discharges issued between December 1, 1941, and June 30, 1945, were issued to black service members. During this time, black people made up just 6.5 percent of army personnel.[10]

For people in needed roles, officers classified those service members suspected of being gay based on three classes of sexual offenses. Male soldiers believed to be gay were court-martialed. Soldiers believed to have engaged in sexual activity with one another due to long periods with no female company were administratively discharged. Soldiers believed to have engaged in a single instance of sexual activity with another man because they were drunk or curious were evaluated for perversion. If none was found, they were returned to duty. This system allowed the military to overlook some gay men and lesbians while maintaining the appearance of sexual purity demanded by US society at that time.

In at least one instance in the US Marines, enlisted men with "homosexual tendencies" serving in the Pacific theater of World War II were offered passage home and a discharge with full benefits if they admitted their sexual orientation. This turned out to be a trick in order to expose gay and lesbian service members. Half of those who opened up about their sexuality were sent to psychiatric hospitals. The other half were incarcerated at military bases before returning to the United States. In some instances, this was referred to as a "queer stockade."[11] Upon their return to the United States, they were stripped of their campaign medals and given an administrative discharge.

DISCUSSION STARTERS

- Do you think it is OK that the identities of LGBTQ soldiers were ignored when the military needed more people? Why or why not?
- Why might an LGBTQ person in the military tell others about their orientation or gender identity?

Alfred Kinsey became an expert on human sex and sexuality.

WARS OF THE
LATE 1900s

J ust three years after the end of World War II, sex researcher Alfred Kinsey published a wide-ranging report on sexuality in the United States. Kinsey's findings suggested that almost one-third of US men had had at least one sexual encounter with another man. In addition, he estimated that 4 percent of men in the United States exclusively preferred same-sex relationships. Those who were against nonheterosexual people used Kinsey's findings as proof that a "homosexual menace" was at work in the United States.[1]

At the same time, the United States and the Soviet Union entered a tense relationship known as the Cold War (1947–1991). People in the United States were afraid of communism in the Soviet Union and thought it would destroy capitalism in the United States. While Soviet and US soldiers did not fight each other directly, the Cold War eventually became a far greater threat to LGBTQ rights than any conflict on the ground.

THE KOREAN WAR AND THE LAVENDER SCARE

Japan ruled Korea prior to the end of World War II. With the defeat of Japan at the end of the war, the United States occupied the southern half of Korea. The Soviet Union occupied the north. In the summer of 1950, the Soviet-backed North Koreans attempted to reunify Korea, and the United States and other allies stepped in to stop them. The United States was concerned that a unified Korea would become a communist nation. This conflict became known as the Korean War (1950–1953).

In 1951, the Uniform Code of Military Justice (UCMJ) made any "unnatural carnal copulation with another person of the same or opposite sex" a crime in all branches of the military.[2] The UCMJ, which defines the military justice system and lists criminal offenses under military law, included

SCREENING FOR SEXUALITY

During World War II, doctors attempted to identify men who were gay by inserting tongue depressors into patients' throats to trigger their gag reflex. It was assumed that gay men would not gag as easily as heterosexual men. Later, doctors conducted hormone tests assuming gay men would have higher levels of estrogen, a female sex hormone, and lower levels of androgen, a male sex hormone, than heterosexual men. This practice was abandoned because it was too expensive and too uncertain.

rules about behaviors for heterosexual service members too. However, the rules were enforced for LGBTQ personnel far more often than for heterosexual service members.

In the early 1950s, the US government fired many gay and lesbian employees. Because homosexuality was viewed as a mental disorder, the government thought these employees could be easily blackmailed by Soviet operatives. In 1953, President Dwight D. Eisenhower signed an executive order banning gay men and lesbians from working for the federal government. Eisenhower said he signed the ban because homosexual employees in the government were a security risk. Hundreds of federal employees were fired simply for being, or being suspected of being, part of the LGBTQ community. This period became known as the lavender scare.

The lavender scare also affected US military personnel. Many investigations targeted women service members for being suspected lesbians. Something as simple as playing softball could be viewed by investigators as cause for suspicion. For many years, playing sports such as softball was a stereotype of lesbians. The investigators even used male and female decoys to try to trap or seduce LGBTQ service members.

Many commanding officers chose to look the other way and focus on the job they had to do. In 1957, an internal navy policy review suggested that there was no basis for the beliefs

LESBIAN SOLDIERS IN THE KOREAN WAR

Maurine McFerrin DeLeo was an air force nurse who served during the Korean War. As a lesbian, she took many precautions to avoid being caught up in the lavender scare. She stated, "They'd send in this gorgeous blonde as a spy to seduce you, and to me that was a crock. . . . We'd have a big laugh about it, you know, because we knew where they were. . . . But we were very careful, very careful."

DeLeo recalls attending a party "with one particular girl [she] was seeing" and another person at the party being hostile to them.[4] At the end of the night, DeLeo received a ride home from two air force pilots whom she did not know. The men drove her to an isolated spot and sexually assaulted her. DeLeo reported the incident to her commanding officer, but no action was taken. DeLeo did not get discharged for being a lesbian. However, she left the service shortly before the end of the Korean War in 1953.

that LGBTQ service members presented security risks or were poor sailors. This review, called the Crittenden Report, stated that many LGBTQ sailors had served honorably and well. It also noted that the navy would be wise to adopt a more progressive mind-set in the matter.

In the first year of the Korean War, the navy discharged 483 service members for homosexuality. By the time the Korean Armistice Agreement was signed in 1953, that number had nearly tripled.[3]

STANDING UP FOR LGBTQ RIGHTS

The Korean War was not the first war where LGBTQ service members were sent home without honorable discharges. But a new gay rights movement, coupled with the bonds created by the common enemy of government persecution, emboldened some veterans in the LGBTQ community to fight back.

One of those people was Frank Kameny, a World War II combat veteran and a graduate of Harvard University. Kameny lost his job with the US Army in the 1950s during the lavender scare. He joined forces with the Mattachine Society, a gay rights organization founded in 1950, to demand that both the military and the US Civil Service Commission stop discriminating against gay citizens.

The Mattachine Society had chapters across the United States.

Another naval aviator, named Jim Estep, also fought back. A different aviator, who was under investigation for homosexuality, unintentionally outed Estep. Officials interrogated Estep and searched his cabin without his knowledge. Estep had to sign a confession before he could leave. He said later, "I thought, 'I don't want to be in an organization that treats me this way.' I don't want them plowing around in the lives of the people I know."[5] Estep went on to mount multiple legal challenges to his dishonorable discharge.

The Korean armistice ended the fighting, but it did not create peace. Even though the communist People's Republic of Korea and the democratic Republic of Korea remained separated, the Cold War did not end. The mid-1950s saw a new theater of conflict in the tiny Southeast Asian nation of Vietnam. Similarly to what happened in Korea, the nation was divided in 1954. One half was communist and the other half was not. The United States entered the country to prevent communist rule from spreading. This was known as the Vietnam War (1955–1975).

As the Vietnam conflict dragged on, it became increasingly unpopular among people in the United States. People held many protests against the Vietnam War. Some anti-war groups suggested that straight men should claim they were homosexual in order to avoid the draft. However, this was not always enough, especially when the military needed more

LGBTQ veterans of the Vietnam War marched openly in the 1987 New York City Veterans Day parade.

soldiers. The pressing need for troops reduced the number of discharges for homosexuality until the war ended in 1975.

VANISHING SOLDIERS

LGBTQ service members faced many challenges. Those who were outed, or identified as gay or lesbian, would suddenly disappear. Their personal items and bedding would be removed without a word. It was as if that soldier had never even existed. Other soldiers who did not disappear would be abused, humiliated, and threatened with a dishonorable discharge or even physical harm. In other instances, LGBTQ soldiers were transferred to special units to endure exceptionally harsh treatment. Military officials hoped that the soldiers,

HOLLYWOOD HOMOPHOBIA

The 1960 movie *Spartacus* tells the story of a Roman slave rebellion. In ancient Rome, sexual relationships between two male soldiers were not considered unusual.

Spartacus was rereleased in 1967 and again in 1991. The 1991 version of the movie contains a bath scene that Hollywood censors deemed inappropriate in both 1960 and 1967. In the scene, Spartacus, played by Lawrence Olivier, attempts to seduce a young male slave played by Tony Curtis. In a 2002 interview, Curtis said the movie was supposed to be a love story between three men. However, executives at Universal Pictures forbade any content that would suggest the men were gay.

particularly men, would toughen up and become heterosexual.

This treatment was dangerous for LGBTQ soldiers. Jess Jessop was a medic in the US Marines during the Vietnam War. He recounted how he ran directly at an enemy machine gunner and attacked him. Jessop was being investigated for homosexuality. He felt it would be better for himself and his family if he died as a hero rather than lived as a gay man. Jessop survived both a military investigation into his sexuality and being wounded in action. He went on to become one of the founders of the San Diego LGBT Center and the Lambda Archives of San Diego.

Bisexual service members faced a similar fate. Private Clifton Francis Arnesen joined the army in 1965 to escape a life of poverty. However, he felt trapped as he hid his bisexuality. Eventually, Arnesen told his commander about his sexuality. Arnesen was quickly put under house arrest and then transferred to the military stockade for interrogation. The interrogators believed that Arnesen was lying about his sexuality to get out of going to Vietnam. They wanted Arnesen to prove that he was bisexual. Desperate to leave the military, Arnesen became involved with another soldier. Both soldiers signed a confession to their activities. Arnesen was court-martialed and sentenced to a year of hard labor. In 1989, he became the first openly bisexual veteran to testify before members of Congress about the suffering of veterans due to LGBTQ-related discharges and discrimination.

Trans soldiers in Vietnam faced different challenges. Janice Covington served in the army in Vietnam in 1965 and 1966. "Back then, I couldn't come out," she said. "I didn't even know if another transgender person existed in this world. We didn't have Internet. We didn't have communication." Covington was wounded in action and nearly captured before being discharged in 1967. She came out in 2004. "We went to battle, we put our lives on the line, we bleed just like they do," she said. "We're people and we have a right to serve the military if we want to, like anybody else."[6]

CONFLICTING CAUSES

The LGBTQ rights movement had been building in the 1960s and 1970s, but it was the Stonewall riots that truly added fuel to the fire. In 1969, a gay bar called the Stonewall Inn in New York City was raided by police. Drag queens and trans women inside fought back against police, which led to a days-long riot in the Greenwich Village neighborhood. This was the start of the modern LGBTQ rights movement.

The Gay Liberation Front (GLF) formed as a result of the Stonewall riots. The GLF openly criticized the war in Vietnam. It did not want gay and lesbian soldiers to be included in

The Gay Liberation Front opposed the military as well as the war in Vietnam.

the military. Instead, it advocated that the military provide gay and lesbian soldiers with honorable discharges. The GLF also encouraged currently serving gay and lesbian soldiers to refuse to fight. However, the GLF's work did not impact many soldiers who were already serving. Those soldiers wanted full inclusion in the military, and they wanted to serve their country with acceptance and honor. It would be many more years before the LGBTQ community united to work for change within the military, rather than outside it.

DISCUSSION STARTERS

- Do you think life was better for LGBTQ people in the military during this time than it was for those in civilian jobs? Why or why not?

- Why might organizations such as the GLF try to persuade gay and lesbian soldiers to refuse to fight?

- Do you think US attitudes toward the Vietnam War affected LGBTQ soldiers in the military? Why or why not?

CHALLENGING THE BAN

The last US troops left Vietnam in 1973. In 1975, a gay service member made the cover of *Time* magazine. Technical Sergeant Leonard Matlovich was the first gay person named on the cover of a magazine in the United States. He was an air force officer who received a Bronze Star and a Purple Heart for his service. He had served three tours in Vietnam and was recovering from injuries he received there when he heard about the 1969 Stonewall riots.

Matlovich reached out to gay activist and military advocate Frank Kameny. Kameny had been looking for someone to challenge the military's ban on LGBTQ soldiers. He needed someone like Matlovich—an active duty gay service member with a perfect record. Together, they challenged the military's ban on homosexual conduct.

The headline under Matlovich's picture on the cover of *Time* read, "I Am a Homosexual."[7] The air force then dismissed Matlovich for his sexuality. Matlovich proceeded to sue the air force over the course of many years. While he did not get the air force to overturn the ban, he did receive back pay and a retroactive promotion because his dismissal was deemed improper. Matlovich continued to fight for gay rights until his death in 1988 from complications related to acquired immunodeficiency syndrome (AIDS). His tombstone in the historic Congressional Cemetery in Washington, DC, has the famous inscription, "When I was in the military they gave me a medal for killing two men and a discharge for loving one."[8]

The inscription on Matlovich's tombstone has become a symbol of the fight for the rights of LGBTQ personnel in the military.

Veteran Perry Watkins served as a co-grand marshal in the 1993 New York City Pride March. He was discharged from the military for his sexuality.

FIGHTING BACK
AND DON'T ASK, DON'T TELL

B y the 1980s, approximately 100,000 LGBTQ service members had been discharged from the military.[1] Some of them became activists. Others began taking their grievances public.

In 1975, US Army staff sergeant Miriam Ben-Shalom became one of the first women drill sergeants in the US Army Reserve. A local television station interviewed her because of her accomplishments. During the interview, Ben-Shalom was asked how it felt to be a lesbian in the military. Ben-Shalom believed a leader should be honest. So she answered the reporter truthfully that she was a lesbian. Ben-Shalom was then dismissed from the US Army.

Ben-Shalom sued the army to reinstate her. She was able to prove in court that the army had violated her First Amendment rights of free speech, freedom of assembly, and privacy because

THE PARRIS ISLAND PURGE

In the late 1980s, the US Marine Corps launched an investigation into lesbian activity at its training facility in Parris Island, South Carolina. Parris Island is the only place for training female recruits, who make up less than 10 percent of marines as of 2016.[2]

The investigation, led by the Naval Investigative Service, began after a staff sergeant under investigation was asked to give up names of women she suspected were lesbians. The woman came up with more than 40 names. Between 1986 and 1988, nearly half of the post's 246 women were questioned about alleged lesbian activities.[3] At that time, engaging in lesbian activity was grounds for discharge from the armed services.

Three female marines were sent to jail, and all told, 65 women eventually left the marines due to the investigation. One officer spoke of an eight-hour interrogation, along with a threat to deny her custody of her child unless she cooperated with investigators.

In 1990, a military appeals court reversed its conviction of a marine corporal who had already spent more than 200 days in jail on charges of engaging in sexual relations with another woman. The court said at the time that two marines sitting on the jury were biased and that the judge had allowed uncorroborated testimony.

the army had fired her based on a statement she made on television. The court ordered the army to reinstate Ben-Shalom. However, the army dismissed the order. Ben-Shalom continued to fight the case in court and eventually was reinstated in 1987.

Army nurse Margarethe Cammermeyer spent nearly three decades in the army and army reserve, including serving in Vietnam from 1967 to 1968. She was dismissed from the army reserve in 1989 when she came out publicly as a lesbian. She won reinstatement and served until she retired in 1997. Cammermeyer commented on the tough road for LGBTQ people in the military and the special challenges faced by lesbian service members. "There is a tremendous amount of lesbian-baiting in the service," she said. "Any straight man who propositions a woman and she's not interested, well, it can't be because he's not attractive. So it must be because she's a lesbian. It's used as a threat all the time."[4]

AT WAR AGAIN

In November 1989, the Cold War was coming to an end. Less than a year later, in August 1990, Iraqi leader Saddam Hussein invaded Kuwait to start the Persian Gulf War (1990–1991). By 1991, more than 500,000 US service members had been deployed to the Middle East, including many LGBTQ personnel.

EMERGENCY AND SITUATIONAL SEXUALITY

In 1982, the DOD adopted regulations stating that a heterosexual person could have sex with someone of the same gender as long as it was due to the circumstances rather than the person's sexual orientation. The regulation formalized a long-standing practice that had been tolerated most often in the navy. Ships at sea meant prolonged periods of time away from women. The military defined *emergency sexuality* as an instance where a heterosexual man might have sex with another man only because there were no women around. Therefore, his sexual orientation would remain heterosexual. This situational sexuality exists in other settings as well, such as prisons, convents, and monasteries, and even boarding schools. It was first acknowledged publicly in an essay published in 1899, which discussed situational sex among men experiencing homelessness in the United States.

As in many prior conflicts, a "stop-loss" order was invoked. This meant that many kinds of legal and administrative actions in the military were suspended once particular units were mobilized for war. These administrative actions included discharges for homosexuality. In essence, it meant LGBTQ service members were protected from discharge as long as they were putting their lives at risk during deployment. Once their deployments were concluded, they could be discharged.

For the increasingly vocal critics of the military ban on LGBTQ service members, the hypocrisy was clear. The Palm Center, an independent public policy research institute, issued a report on the topic. The report stated, "Some observers note that commanders' willingness to send known gays into combat calls into question that rationale that openly gay service undermines the military, since it is during wartime that morale, discipline, and cohesion are most vital."[5]

RATES OF SEXUAL ASSAULT IN THE MILITARY

Margarethe Cammermeyer's comments also shed light on the larger issue of sexual assault in the military. In 2016, more than four in every 100 female service members reported some kind of sexual assault. However, not all assaults were reported. Two-thirds of women who did report an assault suffered some kind of backlash.[6] This sexist culture, combined with homophobia, creates even more problems for any lesbians and bisexual women.

Mark Landes, a graduate of the military academy West Point, experienced this in his service during and after the Persian Gulf War. Once the Persian Gulf War ended, Landes heard rumors of investigations by the army's Criminal Investigation Division. Eventually, he was questioned. "They ask you all kinds of things," Landes recalled. He added:

> They'll actually stop the process of getting a gay man out of the military if a war happens, because they still need you to serve your country, and they're happy for you to serve your country during a time of war. . . . As soon as that threat goes away, they kick you out.[7]

HOW THE ARMY HANDLED THE HIV/AIDS EPIDEMIC

In 1985, the US Army adopted a pragmatic approach to the growing acquired immunodeficiency syndrome (AIDS) epidemic. Though any person can contract the human immunodeficiency virus (HIV), the virus that leads to AIDS, it was often known as the "gay man's disease." Gay men were disproportionately affected by HIV and AIDS.

All 1.2 million active duty and reserve service members were tested annually for HIV. Those service members who tested positive were not discharged, but they were ordered to engage only in safe sex practices. Most service members living with HIV reported fair treatment by their commanders. The army also officially guaranteed confidentiality of results. In one instance, a military pharmacist who publicly announced an available prescription for a common AIDS medication was disciplined for violating this promise of confidentiality.

DON'T ASK, DON'T TELL

In 1992, presidential candidate Bill Clinton promised that he would end the military ban on gay and lesbian service members if he were elected. Once he was elected, however, Clinton ran into strong opposition from several key US senators and top military leaders. In October 1993, Clinton and his opponents arrived at a compromise that came to be known as Don't Ask, Don't Tell (DADT).

Protesters gathered after Don't Ask, Don't Tell went into effect.

Under DADT, the military was not allowed to ask recruits about their sexual orientation. Nonheterosexual service members already in the military were not allowed to talk about their sexual orientation. In addition, their commanding officers were not allowed to ask about their sexual orientations. Trans service members were not covered by DADT and were still subject to expulsion because the military regarded them as mentally ill.

At the time, the United States and Turkey were the only nations within the North Atlantic Treaty Organization (NATO) intergovernmental military alliance that had such a policy regarding service members' sexuality. It also put the United States in the same category as Iran and North Korea in terms of its refusal to allow LGBTQ people to serve in the military.

Neither side liked the compromise of DADT. Opponents of LGBTQ service members feared that the presence of any LGBTQ troops, secret or not, would undermine morale. General Norman Schwarzkopf, who led coalition forces during the Persian Gulf War, testified to senators that allowing openly gay men and women to serve in the military would result in "disheartened" troops.[8] Proponents of LGBTQ service felt the policy still forced LGBTQ soldiers to serve in silence. DADT was far from the complete acceptance they were seeking. As a spokesperson for Senator Edward Kennedy stated, "Members of

HARVEY MILK: GAY SAILOR AND CIVIL RIGHTS PIONEER

Harvey Milk was an early crusader for LGBTQ rights who went on to win public office as an openly gay man. Milk enlisted in the US Navy in 1951 and attended Officer Candidate School in Rhode Island. He then served as a naval diving instructor while stationed in San Diego, California. Milk had attained the rank of lieutenant junior grade by the time he left the navy in 1955 after being officially questioned about his sexuality. He eventually settled in San Francisco, California. There, Milk became active in the city's Castro neighborhood, an LGBTQ-friendly area.

Milk advocated for LGBTQ rights. He was a vocal opponent of the war in Vietnam. After multiple unsuccessful campaigns for public office, Milk was elected as a San Francisco city supervisor in 1977. In his position, he struck down an initiative that would have required dismissing any teacher or school employee found to be either gay or supportive of gay rights. Milk was assassinated in November 1978 by a disgruntled former city supervisor. In 2009, he was posthumously awarded the Presidential Medal of Freedom.

the armed forces, like any other Americans, should be judged by their ability, not by the prejudice of others."[9]

SOCIAL ACCEPTANCE

The gay rights movement was helping to increase social acceptance of LGBTQ people in the United States. Gay veteran Harvey Milk had become a city supervisor for San Francisco in 1977. He was the first openly gay man to be elected to a political office in California. The DOD also had released a report supporting the conclusions of the 1957 Crittenden Report, which had found that gay men and lesbians posed no significant security risk. Meanwhile, trans people largely were still struggling for recognition.

Despite these changes, approximately 13,000 service members were discharged during DADT.[10] Sometimes the reasons were as vague as "unit cohesion." The unit cohesion argument against LGBTQ service arose in the 1980s. The argument stated that regardless of how well any service member performed their duties, the other service members in the unit might be homophobic or simply uncomfortable with that person. As a result, the unit as a whole might experience issues. One general described the homophobia of other service members as a fear that a gay service member might try to initiate unwanted sexual contact. "You've got to understand that a man's biggest fear is a sexual assault," he said.[11]

In 1992, the Government Accounting Office released a report estimating that it cost more than $28,000 to replace each enlisted service member and $120,000 to replace each officer discharged for homosexuality. Those costs did not include the costs of investigating, discharging, and fighting court challenges.[12]

Through it all, LGBTQ soldiers continued to face real threats from discriminatory discharges, enemy combatants, and even their own colleagues. Though allowed to serve, they were not allowed to express their sexual orientation. The situation

In 2003, Barry Winchell's story was turned into the film *Soldier's Girl*. Troy Garity, *back*, played Winchell.

led to what LGBTQ advocate C. Dixon Osburn called "an incubator for hate."[13] Osburn, co-executive director of the group Servicemembers Legal Defense Network (SLDN), said DADT depended on lies and secrecy. Service members could not discuss issues, nor could gay service members be fully who they were.

That incubator for hate reached a boiling point in July 1999. Private First Class Barry Winchell was beaten with a baseball bat by another soldier after it was discovered that he dated a trans woman. Winchell died the following day. For LGBTQ activists, Winchell's murder became a stark reminder of the dangers inherent in DADT.

DISCUSSION STARTERS

- Do you think DADT was a step forward in terms of LGBTQ rights? Why or why not?

- In what ways do your friends or family discuss the people whom they are dating? How do you think it would feel to hide those people from their school or work?

- Do you think unit cohesion is affected by LGBTQ soldiers? Why or why not?

6

THE WAR ON TERROR
AND REPEAL OF DADT

The US military was involved in several small military actions following the Persian Gulf War. However, the next large-scale action would follow the terrorist attacks on the World Trade Center and the Pentagon on September 11, 2001. The United States responded by invading Afghanistan and later Iraq. These military actions became known as the War on Terror.

In 2003, US Army Special Forces member Brian Hughes and army sergeant Robert Stout both served in Iraq. They also came out publicly after their service to advocate for the repeal of DADT. Hughes and Stout argued that though DADT was approved because of unit cohesion, DADT was dividing units. It also discriminated against some members of those units.

They also argued that the policy seemed arbitrary. In 2001, the military had discharged more than 1,200 service members for homosexuality. By 2004, in the midst of multiple conflicts around the world, that number had dropped to 653. Clearly, Hughes and Stout argued, the military found a way to work with LGBTQ soldiers when it was convenient to do so.[1]

Hughes said his decision to come out openly against DADT was inspired by three other brave men. In 2003, retired officers Brigadier General Keith Kerr, Brigadier General Virgil Richard, and Rear Admiral Alan Steinman of the US Coast Guard all came out as gay. All had said DADT had been ineffective and had undermined the military's core values of truth, honor, dignity, respect, and integrity.

THE ROLE OF CIVIL COURTS

LGBTQ service members who believe they have been discriminated against are advised to seek action through official military channels. This process typically involves submitting a complaint via the chain of command. If the military rules against the service member, there are few remaining options. As a result, service members may take the cases to civil courts once they leave the military.

Civil courts have played a role in several key discrimination cases involving LGBTQ veterans. Both Leonard Matlovich and Miriam Ben-Shalom took their discharge cases to court. In September 2010, a US district court judge ruled DADT was unconstitutional due to its violation of LGBTQ service members' First and Fifth Amendment rights. The judge in the case issued an injunction to stop enforcement of DADT. However, the Obama administration asked her to stay, or delay, her ruling due to potential disruptions to ongoing military operations. Congress then voted to repeal DADT later that year.

In 2010, activists and gay veterans handcuffed themselves to the fence outside the White House to protest DADT.

The officers also spoke of the personal hardship created by DADT. "I was denied the opportunity to share my life with a loved one, to have a family, to do all the things that heterosexual Americans take for granted," said Steinman. "That's the sacrifice I made to serve my country."[2]

Added Richard, "There are gays and lesbians who want to serve honorably and with integrity, but have been forced to compromise."[3] He said ending DADT was a matter of honor and integrity.

THE END OF DADT

In 2007, presidential candidate Barack Obama made a pledge that if he were elected president, he would repeal DADT. In 2010, President Obama made good on this promise. Congress approved the repeal of DADT in December 2010, and it went into effect in September 2011. Service members could no longer be discharged due to sexual orientation. In addition, those who had been discharged were allowed to reenter.

The end of DADT led to many changes for LGBTQ soldiers. Under DADT, air force major Adrianna Vorderbruggen had not been allowed to talk about her pregnancy and the birth of her son. Upon the repeal of DADT, she married her wife and became one

EQUAL MARRIAGE RIGHTS AND LGBTQ SERVICE MEMBERS AND VETERANS

The right of same-sex couples to legally marry and have that marriage recognized has unique implications for LGBTQ couples in the military. Prior to the repeal of DADT, even same-sex couples who *had* obtained a legal marriage were unable to acknowledge their spouses, as doing so would set them up for discharge. Additionally, after the repeal of DADT, same-sex married couples who transferred to a different military base might move to a state that did not recognize their marriage. The Supreme Court case *Obergefell v. Hodges* cleared the way for all same-sex couples, including those in the military, to have their marriages recognized. This is regardless of state of residence.

of the first openly gay service members to get married. Sadly, Vorderbruggen was killed in 2015 while serving in Afghanistan. However, because of the repeal of DADT, her wife and son were recognized by the military as family. They were given military survivor benefits.

PETITIONING THEIR DISCHARGE

For Helen James, military service was a matter of family tradition. Her great-grandfather served in the Union Army during the American Civil War. Her father served in World War I. She watched relatives leave the Pennsylvania farming community where she lived to fight in World War II. It was no surprise then that James enlisted in the US Air Force in 1952.

James recalls that military life suited her, and she enjoyed the chance to meet new people from around the country. By 1955, James had already earned a promotion and applied to be a commissioned officer. Then the trouble began.

At first it was just rumors. The rumors stated that the air force's Office of Special Investigations was hunting for gay and lesbian service members. James, along with several other lesbians on her base on Long Island, New York, began to notice odd things. Upon returning to their barracks, it appeared that their rooms had been searched. Sometimes when they were off of the base, they felt as though they were being followed.

DISCRIMINATION AGAINST LGBTQ MILITARY SPOUSES

Historically, heterosexual spouses of active duty military personnel have been entitled to nearly 100 military benefits, including health care, housing allowances, and survivor benefits. LGBTQ service members were by default denied those benefits before and during DADT, as any attempt to marry someone of the same sex would expose them for dismissal.

Military benefits for same-sex spouses became a reality after the repeal of DADT and the Supreme Court decision on Section 3 of the Defense of Marriage Act (DOMA). This historic court decision in June 2013 cleared the way for including same-sex spouses in military benefits programs. Even more importantly, the decision meant same-sex spouses were eligible for federal spousal benefits even if they were stationed in a state that did not recognize their marriages. The military went a step further to permit same-sex couples to take leave in order to travel to a state where they could legally marry.

Despite these efforts, the same situation did not apply to veterans. Prior to the *Obergefell v. Hodges* decision in 2015, same-sex spouses of veterans could receive only limited veterans' benefits if they lived in states where same-sex marriage was illegal.

Navy veteran Joan Darrah, *right*, and her spouse, Lynne Kennedy, were able to receive veterans' spousal benefits after the Supreme Court decision on the Defense of Marriage Act (DOMA) in 2013.

Things happened quickly after that. James was one of a number of lesbian service members who were arrested and interrogated. She ultimately received an undesirable discharge. That type of discharge began a chain of discrimination that followed James wherever she went. It meant she could not pay for her schooling through the GI Bill. The GI Bill refers to several laws that provide funds for college tuition, home-buying loans,

Many LGBTQ veterans seek to change their discharges to honorable discharges.

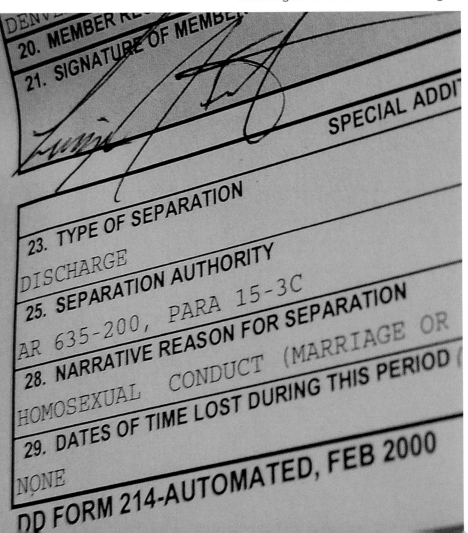

20. MEMBER RE...

21. SIGNATURE OF MEMBER

SPECIAL ADDI

23. TYPE OF SEPARATION

DISCHARGE

25. SEPARATION AUTHORITY

AR 635-200, PARA 15-3C

28. NARRATIVE REASON FOR SEPARATION

HOMOSEXUAL CONDUCT (MARRIAGE OR

29. DATES OF TIME LOST DURING THIS PERIOD (

NONE

DD FORM 214-AUTOMATED, FEB 2000

and other benefits for veterans.

James recalled that one of the hardest things was right before she left the base, when she found that someone had cut the buttons off her uniform. "That's how they disgrace you, so you can't wear your uniform, so you can't belong to the United States military," she said.[4]

At age 90, James petitioned to have her discharge changed from undesirable to honorable. In doing so, she joined a growing number of LGBTQ veterans seeking the change, which is required to access veterans' benefits.

In addition to the lack of benefits, LGBTQ veterans dealt with shame from their undesirable discharges. Private Donald Hallman was kicked out of the military in 1955 at the age of 21. In a 2015 interview, the then 82-year-old said he had told no

SPECIAL TRAINING FOR MILITARY CHAPLAINS

Many proponents of DADT warned that the repeal of the policy would cause military chaplains who did not agree with same-sex relationships to exit the service. The armed services heeded the warning and began training chaplains regarding the repeal of the ban. Chaplains who could not follow the policy were offered an opportunity to voluntarily depart from the service.

As it turned out, most military chaplains did not report that their ministries were conflicted or constrained. While a small number of chaplains did seek voluntary release, most continued their service in the military.

one of the incident and had burned all of his military records except for one dog tag that he hid. "I hid it because it would have ruined my life," he said.[5] Similarly, air force member Joshua Hoffman recalled an interrogation and subsequent discharge for homosexuality in 1986. "I was kicked out of my job, my church, my housing: I had nothing," Hoffman said. "It took a long time to realize I deserved respect."[6] When Hoffman received a reclassification of his discharge to honorable, he posted it on his Facebook page and became open about his story.

LAMBDA LEGAL

In 1973, Lambda Legal became the first nonprofit legal organization fighting for the rights of people in the LGBTQ community. Since then, volunteer attorneys with the group have been challenging discrimination by the military against LGBTQ soldiers.

Lambda Legal successfully fought for military benefits for married same-sex couples. It continues to fight for the rights of military personnel discharged on the basis of sexual orientation between World War II and the end of DADT. Other work areas for Lambda Legal include advocating for trans people in the military.

James, Hallman, and Hoffman are among nearly 500 service members who have requested an upgrade of their discharge status since the repeal of DADT. Government records indicate approximately 80 percent of the requests have been approved.[7]

In addition to the emotional toll of the shame and of losing out on important benefits, the discharges also cost LGBTQ

Veterans can attend job fairs to find new careers after they leave the military.

service members government jobs and other employment opportunities. While LGBTQ status is not the only reason for undesirable discharges, some civilian employers have nonetheless adopted policies that exclude all veterans with such discharges from consideration. In addition to LGBTQ veterans, such undesirable discharges—commonly called "bad paper"—can ensnare veterans discharged for other discriminatory reasons, including race, disability, and gender. This problem is compounded by a general lack of understanding among civilian employers of the military discharge process. In reality, dishonorable discharges are rare, and the military now works to avoid them whenever possible. For example, there were approximately 207,000 military discharges in 2014. Of those, only 2 percent were other than honorable discharges, 0.3 percent were bad conduct discharges, and 0.0007 percent were dishonorable discharges.[8]

RIGHTS FOR TRANSGENDER SOLDIERS

While the repeal of DADT protected soldiers based on their sexuality, it did not include soldiers who may be discharged for their gender identity. Trans soldiers continue advocating for their right to enlist in the military. Kristin Beck is a trans woman and a veteran US Navy SEAL. She received a Bronze Star, a Purple Heart, and 27 other medals during her service. She was deployed 13 times to areas of conflict.

Beck is outspoken in her beliefs about trans service members. She maintains that a professional unit with great leadership wouldn't have a problem with someone being trans. She is also aware of the challenges of being forced to hide one's identity. According to Beck, the SEALs were the "toughest of the tough."[9] She recalls thinking that she could stop being a trans person if she could succeed at that level. Now, she is more comfortable being who she is. Another trans veteran, retired sergeant major Jennifer Long, talked about the need for all people in the United States to have the right to serve. She stated:

> Today with an all-volunteer military, the requirement of inclusiveness is . . . greater because force size and the mix of specialties will require service members and leaders who will be able to operate in any political, cultural or environmental climate. We all have the right to defend freedom.[10]

DISCUSSION STARTERS

- Do you think the military should regulate sexuality and gender identity separately? Why or why not?

- Why might someone petition their discharge many decades after they left the military?

- Did the end of DADT affect anyone you know? What about people in your community?

Some LGBTQ servicepeople find that their peers are more accepting of their gender identity and sexuality than civilians.

LIFE AS AN
LGBTQ SOLDIER

Some LGBTQ people have found that life in the military can be better than civilian life. Many people attribute this to the military's need for people from a wide range of backgrounds. Defending the United States from its enemies requires a broad pool of talent. The result is a melting pot of people working toward shared goals.

Such was the experience of one gay service member who shared his story with *Mel* magazine in a July 2017 article. "I came to find that the military, as a whole, was actually more socially progressive than society," he said. He added,

> Sure, there were some guys who were uncomfortable, but I assumed that was the result of where they came from, and maybe never having met an openly gay person before. But the military challenges this kind of thinking because it's a convergence of everyone—it's the whole country mixed together.[1]

LGBTQ? YES. VETERAN? NO.

Despite the repeal of DADT, professionals working with LGBTQ veterans are seeing those veterans struggle to rejoin the LGBTQ and veteran communities. "Most LGBTQ vets that I've worked with identify much more closely with the LGBTQ community than the veteran community," said Nathaniel Boehme with the Oregon Department of Veterans' Affairs. "I run into vets who tell me, 'That's part of my life I never want to talk about again.'"[4] Boehme and others have found some success working to bring veterans and LGBTQ groups together to address common challenges, such as upgrading their discharge paperwork to open up new opportunities. This approach has helped address the homelessness and addiction issues that tend to be more prominent in the LGBTQ veteran community.

Saige Santana, a bisexual marine, reported the same thing on his YouTube channel. "You're going to get so many different people from all walks of life . . . so you get a lot of different morals and ethics coming your way," he said. "You will get a lot of people who are homophobic, and you are going to get a lot of people who are going to hate you for no reason at all. . . . You're just going to have to roll with it."[2] Santana added that some heterosexual people are uncomfortable living in close quarters with LGBTQ colleagues, but most are just curious. Santana says people in the military are recognized by peers more for their work than for anything else. "You all are fighting the same fight and you all are on the same team," he said.[3]

These different morals and ethics can create challenges, however. Air force service member and lesbian

Servicepeople rely on other members of their unit to aid them in combat on other missions.

Ashley Carothers worked with many LGBTQ service members at OutServe-Servicemembers Legal Defense Network (SLDN), a nonprofit group that advocates on behalf of LGBTQ military personnel. Carothers spoke with LGBTQ service members who were uncomfortable discussing their sexuality with some members of their units. "You just know not to converse with those individuals and talk about your personal life," she said.[5]

Another OutServe-SLDN leader, Matthew Hardwig, acknowledges that some service members do still make negative comments about the fact that he is gay. Now, however, he makes sure that he reports those situations to his superior officers. "I can't tell the people in my chapter to report it if I'm not going to do it myself," he said.[6]

LIBRARY OF CONGRESS'S VETERANS HISTORY PROJECT

The US Library of Congress began its Veterans History Project in 2000 to capture the experiences of veterans and educate new generations about the realities of war from World War II to present-day conflicts. In 2016, the project expanded to include stories from LGBTQ veterans as a part of a new installment. The new addition, "Speaking Out: LGBT Veterans," shares stories not only of active duty experiences but also of advocacy work on behalf of LGBTQ soldiers and veterans.

LINGERING HESITATION

Many LGBTQ service members who report an overall positive experience often note that they are accepted as they are by their units. An anonymous soldier spoke about the first time he told his colleagues he was gay. It was two days into basic training. He said:

The conversation made its way over to me, and they asked if I had a girlfriend. I took a moment and then said, "I have

After the repeal of DADT, same-sex spouses and their families can live together in military base housing.

a boyfriend." They paused for what felt like the longest second of my life. Then the general reaction was nothing more than, "Oh, that's cool."[7]

He added that by the end of basic training, not everyone knew he was a gay man, meaning it had not been big enough news to share widely.

Ashley Broadway-Mack, president of the American Military Partner Association, is married to Lieutenant Colonel Heather Mack. Broadway-Mack met her wife during DADT. They had no choice but to live off of the military base if they wanted to live together. They said they were roommates or cousins instead of partners. Now that they can live openly as a couple, Broadway-Mack says, their life is much like that of any heterosexual military couple with one exception. "We don't mean to be, but I guess we were programmed for so long, we're just not touchy-feely people outside of our house," she said. "I still to this day feel like, is somebody watching me? And I have to go, no we're good."[8]

HAPPY TO SERVE

A lesbian staff sergeant named Jennifer said the challenges of being a woman are more relevant than the challenges of being gay in the military. "The military is still by far a man's world," said Jennifer. "I believe there are instances when women do not get jobs above a man simply because they are a woman. I think there will always be some men that see women as weaker . . . we just have to find ways to overcome this."[9]

However, other women interviewed by the LGBTQ website After Ellen said a life in the military was a good choice for them. According to Sarah,

The military is an incredibly diverse organization, so you won't be alone. And you will meet people who you will literally trust your life with and you will experience things that you just can't anywhere else.[10]

BEING A WOMAN IN THE MILITARY

Military service for women, whether straight or gay, continues to be more of a challenge than it is for men. Lesbians in particular face higher-than-average levels of discrimination. In a 1997 report, the SLDN explained that one result of DADT was that women who turned down sexual advances by men, or reported sexual abuse, were accused of being lesbians. In addition, SLDN reported that women who were top performers in nontraditional fields also faced ongoing speculation and rumors that they were lesbians.

DOD statistics from 1983 to 1988 show women were discharged for homosexual conduct at a rate nearly ten times that of their gay male colleagues.[11] The situation forced some LGBTQ service members to take drastic measures. Patty Duwel was a naval officer in the mid-1980s when she married a gay colleague to escape being investigated for homosexual activity.

In April 2017, former marine Erika Butner testified to the Democratic Women's Working Group. She stated that all female marines were expected to endure sexual harassment from their male colleagues. Butner said they were told they could be labeled as a whore or a lesbian if they reported their male colleagues for harassment.

Adds another interviewee, Anne, "So much has changed since when I first joined. I applaud any woman who is ready to step up and challenge the men." And even Jennifer notes, "It was the best decision I have ever made in my life. The military has instilled dedication, integrity and loyalty in me and I will always be thankful for my choice to join."[12]

For many LGBTQ service members, the end of DADT has created new, stronger bonds with their colleagues. Shane Ortega, a retired marine who served in Iraq and Afghanistan, talked about the stress that DADT created in the minds of LGBTQ people. "Think about being an American spy in Russia and how difficult that would be," he said. "You have to be perfect in every sense of the word. You have to always question people around you. You can never relax. You have to always

NO MORE WITCH HUNTS

In June 2015, Secretary of Defense Ashton Carter announced that any commander suspected of discriminating against a service member due to their sexual orientation would be investigated. The rule marked a dramatic reversal of decades of witch hunts, during which some military commanders employed secret searches, surveillance, informers, scare tactics, and other investigatory procedures to find and discharge LGBTQ service members. Carter stated that soldiers would be protected from discrimination based on their sexuality by the Pentagon's equal opportunity policy. However, this policy did not include protections for soldiers against discrimination based on gender identity.

think ahead. And you have to always be observant and aware of yourself and your surroundings."[13]

Ortega said the openness that is common now is especially important in a world that relies on trust and knowing who has your back. "In high-kinetic situations where you're exchanging rounds, you want to know the person standing next to you, because that's all that counts at that moment."[14]

DISCUSSION STARTERS

- How might LGBTQ soldiers have a more positive experience in the military than in their hometowns?

- Do you think that men and women in the LGBTQ community have different experiences in the military?

After Trump's attempted ban on trans servicepeople, trans veterans visited military memorials at Arlington National Cemetery.

THE FUTURE OF LGBTQ PEOPLE IN THE MILITARY

President Trump's attempted 2017 ban on transgender service members took many people by surprise, including officials at the DOD. White House spokespeople said the Trump administration did not yet know what would happen to trans soldiers currently serving in the military. Officials also said an implementation plan for the directive had not yet been developed. In the meantime, polling shows that the majority of people in the United States oppose the ban and support trans people serving openly in the military.

Shortly after announcement of the ban, several civil rights groups supporting equal rights for trans soldiers filed lawsuits to block the ban. The lawsuits challenged the ban as unconstitutional. As a result, multiple federal judges halted implementation of the ban. However, in January 2019, the Supreme Court allowed the ban to remain in place while the

CHELSEA MANNING: MILITARY WHISTLE-BLOWER

Chelsea Manning joined the military in 2007. She was sent to Iraq in 2009 as a military intelligence analyst. While in Iraq, Manning had access to a significant amount of classified information. This included information she found troubling, such as videos of unarmed civilians being shot and killed. Manning reached out to several key news media outlets to call attention to the situation, with no success. Eventually, she shared the information with WikiLeaks.

Manning was dishonorably discharged and sentenced to 35 years in prison. Her sentence was the harshest one in the history of military whistle-blowers. A whistle-blower is an informant who shares information about an organization's activities. While Manning was not convicted of aiding the enemy, she was found guilty of espionage, theft, and computer fraud. Many people believed she had been treated unjustly for doing something she believed was right.

Manning, who is transgender, began transitioning while incarcerated in a male military prison. While her gender identity was not a factor in her court case, transitioning in a prison created many challenges. Manning credits letters from veterans, trans young people, parents, politicians, and artists for helping her through the challenging times. After she served seven years, President Obama commuted her sentence in early 2017.

lower courts decided whether the ban was unconstitutional. According to Heather Marie Stur, a professor of military history at the University of Southern Mississippi, Trump is the "first president to overturn the integration of a minority group into the military." She adds:

The military has been a progressive force for equality, even if its motive for incorporating minorities has been the pragmatic need for the best soldiers. By annulling the right of transgender personnel to serve openly, Trump is undoing a 70-year tradition of thinking rationally about military readiness.[1]

MORE-EQUAL OPPORTUNITY

As the lawsuits against the ban on trans service members remain in the court system as of 2019, the future of their military service remains unresolved until those cases are concluded. The situation for gay, lesbian, and bisexual service members is more defined, as all can now serve openly in the military. Military leaders have committed to equal opportunity for all in their ranks, regardless of sexual orientation. In its recognition of Pride Month in 2017, the army's STAND-TO! web platform for internal communications acknowledged the benefits of these policies. It stated, "The Army values the honorable service of all its Soldiers and strongly embraces diversity as a way to create a system that maximizes individual talents, increases morale and greatly enhances military effectiveness."[2]

However, some challenges still remain. Policies of the US Department of Veterans Affairs (VA) prohibit trans veterans from accessing gender-affirming surgeries. The American Medical Association, American Psychological Association, American Academy of Family Physicians, and American College of Obstetricians and Gynecologists all have issued public statements concluding that this transition-related care is both medically necessary and an appropriate treatment for gender dysphoria. In 2018, the VA opened a public comment period for people to discuss transition-related care. The Human Rights Campaign, a major LGBTQ rights advocacy group, worked with more than 2,000 LGBTQ people and allies to submit comments in support of changing this policy.

Beginning in October 2018, another Trump administration policy, Deploy or Get Out!, threatened the status of soldiers living with HIV. The policy directed the military to discharge service members who cannot be deployed outside the United States for more than 12 months. Because an earlier policy prohibits service members living with HIV to deploy overseas, the new policy makes it impossible for approximately 1,200 service members living with HIV to comply.[3] It also rules out military service for anyone with HIV.

Opponents of the ban, including one officer who filed a lawsuit against it,

LGBTQ PERSONNEL AT RISK FOR SEXUAL TRAUMA

Despite the repeal of DADT, LGBTQ military personnel continued to fight sexual orientation discrimination. A doctoral student at the City University of New York undertook an internet survey of more than 250 LGBTQ service members in 2012–2013. The survey indicated women and men faced similar levels of sexual orientation discrimination. However, they reported more threats and intimidation, vandalism, and physical assault outside of the military than within. In addition, women were more likely than men to report experiences of sexual harassment.[4]

say the policy does not recognize advances in treating HIV. Proponents, including former defense secretary Jim Mattis, said the policy is intended to ensure that no service members are deployed more than others. The policy also seeks to encourage service members who wish to remain in uniform to maintain deployable status, as well as to reduce the nondeployable portion of the military to no more than 5 percent of all service members.[5]

A STRONGER ALLIANCE

One outcome of the ban on transgender servicepeople in the military has been the prospect of a more aligned force advocating for LGBTQ rights in the future. Prior movements seeking greater equality for LGBTQ people tended to split between sexual orientation and gender identity. For example, in the 2000s, some advocates for a federal law banning employment discrimination based on

TRANSMILITARY TELLS ALL

English filmmaker Fiona Dawson is bisexual and an advocate for LGBTQ rights. She worked to help repeal DADT, and about a year later, she realized transgender service members still faced an uncertain future. Dawson began collecting the video stories of transgender military personnel. In 2015, she received a commission from the *New York Times* to craft those stories into a short-length documentary film, *TransMilitary*. It has been one of the most-viewed pieces on the *New York Times* website and was nominated for an Emmy. In 2018, *TransMilitary* was turned into a feature-length film that was shown at festivals.

Military recruits come together and learn how to work toward a common goal regardless of unit members' sexual orientations and gender identities.

sexual orientation were reluctant to include discrimination based on gender identity in their proposed bill. In addition, some advocacy groups focused on enacting change via the legal system. Others preferred to seek change through political action.

As the movement to allow open military service by gays and lesbians succeeded with the repeal of DADT, however, some of the organizations fighting for those rights began to include trans service members in their goals. In particular, the SLDN reorganized after DADT was repealed and began advocating for service rights for the trans community. Likewise, the trans ban in the military brought together both legal and political advocacy groups to challenge the policy.

As in military campaigns themselves, a common goal has united multiple, separate forces. Many commentators have noted the important role of the military in fostering social change. The military has been at the forefront of such landmark policies as allowing women in combat, integrating soldiers of color, and enforcing equal opportunities and treatment. As one of the remaining societal melting pots in an increasingly divided nation, it is likely that the military will continue to play an important role in advancing greater understanding and acceptance of LGBTQ people.

DISCUSSION STARTERS

- Why might the Supreme Court overturn an injunction about the ban on trans soldiers? How does that affect trans people currently serving in the military?

- Why might people file lawsuits against the military in civil court? How have these cases helped LGBTQ rights?

- Should the military pay for transition-related care? Why or why not?

ESSENTIAL FACTS

SIGNIFICANT EVENTS

- In 1920, homosexuality among members of the military was criminalized as an offense worthy of court-martial.

- The Cold War's worries over potential communist spies created the persecution of gay and lesbian service members during the lavender scare. This persecution lasted from the 1950s into the 1990s.

- Don't Ask, Don't Tell (DADT) was the compromise reached by Congress in 1993. It permitted gay and lesbian soldiers to serve in the military but required them to stay closeted. DADT wasn't repealed until 2010.

- In 2016, the Obama administration ended a previous ban on transgender soldiers serving openly in the military. However, in 2017 President Trump tweeted that trans soldiers would no longer be allowed to serve openly. While several lower courts placed injunctions on the ban while people filed cases in civil courts, in 2019 the Supreme Court ruled that the ban could continue until it ruled on the legality of the ban.

KEY PLAYERS

- President Bill Clinton signed DADT into law in 1993. While he campaigned as a pro-LGBTQ candidate, once in office he restricted rights for many LGBTQ Americans.

- Adrianna Vorderbruggen was an air force major and one of the first people to marry her partner after the repeal of DADT in 2010. She was also one of the first openly lesbian people to be killed in combat while serving in Afghanistan.

- President Barack Obama signed the repeal of DADT. His administration also created a policy that would allow trans soldiers to serve openly in the US military.

IMPACT ON SOCIETY

Throughout US history, LGBTQ people have been impacted by social and military policy. An all-voluntary military helped usher in a new era in which soldiering was a professional choice as opposed to a national necessity. In addition, it heightened the need for new pools of talent, including diverse forces able to meet the increasingly complex demands of a volatile, complex, and unpredictable world. World War II opened the door to a landmark shift in cultural attitudes regarding everything from sexuality to women's rights. Soldiers' exposure to new people and new experiences set the groundwork for the seismic shifts in how gender and sexuality are perceived now versus before the war. The trans community's struggles have only recently received widespread attention. In attempting to ban trans service members, President Trump called greater attention to their concerns, inadvertently prompting a concerted effort that united the full LGBTQ community—along with advocates—in a way not before experienced.

QUOTE

"When I was in the military they gave me a medal for killing two men and a discharge for loving one."

—*Inscription on Leonard Matlovich's tombstone*

GLOSSARY

CISGENDER (CIS)
Having a gender identity that matches the sex they were assigned at birth.

COURT-MARTIAL
To try members of the military in a special court because they are accused of breaking military law.

DISCHARGE
To formally end military service.

DRAFT
A system in which people of a certain age are required to register for military service.

DRAG QUEEN
A performer, usually a cisgender man, who dresses as a woman for the purpose of entertaining others at bars, clubs, or other events.

DRILL
An exercise done to practice military skills.

GENDER DYSPHORIA
The distress caused by having a gender identity that does not match the sex assigned at birth.

GENDER IDENTITY
A person's perception of their gender, which may or may not correspond with the sex they were assigned at birth.

HOMOPHOBIA
Fear of and hostility toward gay people.

PERJURY
The crime of telling a lie in a court of law after promising to tell the truth.

PRIDE
An annual parade or protest for LGBTQ rights.

SEXUAL ORIENTATION
A person's identity in relation to the gender(s) they find sexually attractive.

TRANSGENDER (TRANS)
Having a gender identity that does not match the sex they were assigned at birth.

UNIT
A group in the military that is part of a larger group.

ADDITIONAL RESOURCES

SELECTED BIBLIOGRAPHY

Benes, Ross. "How Exclusion from the Military Strengthened Gay Identity in America." *Rolling Stone*, 3 Oct. 2016, rollingstone.com. Accessed 12 Dec. 2018.

Gurung, Sitaji, et al. "Despite Policy Changes, LGBT Military Personnel Still Experience Sexual Trauma and Discrimination." *CUNY Graduate School of Public Health and Health Policy*, 8 Jan. 2018, sph.cuny.edu. Accessed 12 Dec. 2018.

FURTHER READINGS

Harris, Duchess, and Kristin Marciniak. *Being Transgender in America*. Abdo, 2020.

Head, Honor. *Trans Global: Transgender Then, Now and Around the World*. Franklin Watts, 2018.

ONLINE RESOURCES

To learn more about LGBTQ service in the armed forces, please visit **abdobooklinks.com** or scan this QR code. These links are routinely monitored and updated to provide the most current information available.

MORE INFORMATION

For more information on this subject, contact or visit the following organizations:

AMERICAN MILITARY PARTNER ASSOCIATION
1725 I St. NW, Suite 300
Washington, DC 20006
militarypartners.org

The American Military Partner Association is a national organization that advocates for LGBTQ military families.

HUMAN RIGHTS CAMPAIGN
1640 Rhode Island Ave. NW
Washington, DC 20036-3278
hrc.org

The Human Rights Campaign (HRC) is an advocacy group and civil rights organization for LGBTQ people.

SPEAKING OUT: LGBT VETERANS
loc.gov/vets/stories

Speaking Out: LGBT Veterans is a collection of narratives of LGBT soldiers in the Veterans History Project, hosted by the Library of Congress. People can view stories, videos, and images of LGBT veterans from World War II to the present.

SOURCE NOTES

CHAPTER 1. NEW ADMINISTRATION

1. Jeremy Diamond. "Trump to Reinstate US Military Ban on Transgender People." *CNN*, 26 July 2017, cnn.com. Accessed 21 Jan. 2019.

2. Debra Bell. "Arguing For and Against Women in Combat." *US News & World Report*, 15 May 2013, usnews.com. Accessed 21 Jan. 2019.

3. Agnes Gereben Schaefer et al. *Assessing the Implications of Allowing Transgender Personnel to Serve Openly*. RAND Corporation, 2016, rand.org. Accessed 21 Jan. 2019.

4. Editorial Board. "A Growing Problem for the Military Transgender Ban: Facts." *New York Times*, 29 Apr. 2018, nytimes.com. Accessed 21 Jan. 2019.

5. Corinne Segal. "As Trump's Ban Plays Out in Court, America's First Openly Transgender Recruits Are Joining the Military." *PBS News Hour*, 9 Mar. 2018, pbs.org. Accessed 21 Jan. 2019.

6. Helene Cooper. "Critics See Echoes of 'Don't Ask, Don't Tell' in Military Transgender Ban." *New York Times*, 28 Mar. 2018, nytimes.com. Accessed 21 Jan. 2019.

7. Randy Shilts. *Conduct Unbecoming: Gays and Lesbians in the U.S. Military*. St. Martin's Griffin, 1994. 163–164.

CHAPTER 2. LGBTQ SOLDIERS IN THE 1700s AND 1800s

1. Rebecca Nagle. "The Healing History of Two-Spirit, a Term That Gives LGBTQ Natives a Voice." *HuffPost*, 30 June 2018, huffingtonpost.com. Accessed 21 Jan. 2019.

2. Laura Mills. "Osh-Tisch, the Warrior." *Making Queer History*, 8 Jul. 2016, makingqueerhistory.com. Accessed 21 Jan. 2019.

3. "Constructing the Hetero, Homo, Bi System." *OutHistory*, 3 Nov. 2016, outhistory.org. Accessed 21 Jan. 2019.

4. Irene Monroe. "America's Gay Confederate and Union Soldiers." *HuffPost*, 22 Apr. 2011, huffingtonpost.com. Accessed 21 Jan. 2019.

5. Steve Hendrix. "A History Lesson for Trump: Transgender Soldiers Served in the Civil War." *Washington Post*, 25 Aug. 2017, washingtonpost.com. Accessed 21 Jan. 2019.

6. Hendrix, "A History Lesson for Trump."

7. Hendrix, "A History Lesson for Trump."

CHAPTER 3. LGBTQ SOLDIERS IN THE WORLD WARS

1. Craig A. Rimmerman. *The Lesbian and Gay Movements: Assimilation or Liberation?* Westview, 2015. 78.

2. Donna Patricia Ward. "FDR's Investigation of Homosexuals at the Army and Navy YMCA in Rhode Island." *History Collection*, n.d., historycollection.co. Accessed 21 Jan. 2019.

3. Nancy Hedin. "Far from the 'Well of Loneliness' Pride Feature: Is There a Lesbian Writers' Community in Minnesota?" *Minnesota Women's Press*, n.d., womenspress.com. Accessed 21 Jan. 2019.

4. GLBT Historical Society. "World War II." *Out Ranks*, 17 Apr. 2018, glbthistory.org. Accessed 21 Jan. 2019.

5. GLBT Historical Society, "World War II."

6. John Costello. *Virtue under Fire: How World War II Changed Our Social and Sexual Attitudes*. Little, Brown, 1985. 103.

7. "Nazi Persecution of Homosexuals." *United States Holocaust Memorial Museum*, n.d., ushmm.org. Accessed 21 Jan. 2019.

8. Katya Cengel. "Rosie the LGBT Riveter." *Newsweek*, 12 June 2014, newsweek.com. Accessed 21 Jan. 2019.

9. Allan Bérubé. *Coming Out under Fire: The History of Gay Men and Women in World War II*. U of North Carolina P, 1990. 180.

10. Phillip McGuire, ed. *Taps for a Jim Crow Army: Letters from Black Soldiers in World War II*. UP of Kentucky, 2015. 146.

11. Costello, *Virtue under Fire*, 117

CHAPTER 4. WARS OF THE LATE 1900s

1. Steve Estes. *Ask and Tell: Gay and Lesbian Veterans Speak Out*. U of North Carolina P, 2009. 29–31.

2. Adam Serwer. "Why the Military Still Bans Sodomy." *MSNBC*, 20 June 2013, msnbc.com. Accessed 21 Jan. 2019.

3. Estes, *Ask and Tell*, 30.

4. Estes, *Ask and Tell*, 49.

5. Estes, *Ask and Tell*, 58.

6. Matt Kwong. "What These Transgender Veterans Think about Trump's U.S. Trans Troop Ban." *CBC News*, 27 July 2017, cbc.ca. Accessed 21 Jan. 2019.

7. Lily Rothman. "How a Closeted Air Force Sergeant Became the Face of Gay Rights." *Time*, 8 Sept. 2015, time.com. Accessed 21 Jan. 2019.

8. Hayley Miller. "40 Years Since Leonard Matlovich's Time Magazine Cover." *Human Rights Campaign*, 8 Sept. 2015, hrc.org. Accessed 21 Jan. 2019.

CHAPTER 5. FIGHTING BACK AND DON'T ASK, DON'T TELL

1. Ross Benes. "How Exclusion from the Military Strengthened Gay Identity in America." *Rolling Stone*, 3 Oct. 2016, rollingstone.com. Accessed 21 Jan. 2019.

2. George M. Reynolds and Amanda Shendruk. "Demographics of the US Military." *Council on Foreign Relations*, 24 Apr. 2018, cfr.org. Accessed 21 Jan. 2019.

3. Allyson Collins et al. *Uniform Discrimination: The "Don't Ask, Don't Tell" Policy of the US Military*. Human Rights Watch, 2003. 7.

4. Catherine S. Manegold. "The Odd Place of Homosexuality in the Military." *New York Times*, 18 Apr. 1993, nytimes.com. Accessed 21 Jan. 2019.

5. Nathaniel Frank. "Research Note on Pentagon Practice of Sending Known Gays and Lesbians to War." *Palm Center*, 1 Jul. 2007, palmcenter.org. Accessed 21 Jan. 2019.

6. Dan Lamothe. "Sexual Assault on Both Men and Women in the Military Is Declining, Pentagon Survey Finds." *Washington Post*, 1 Mar. 2017, washingtonpost.com. Accessed 21 Jan. 2019.

7. Steve Estes. *Ask and Tell: Gay and Lesbian Veterans Speak Out*. U of North Carolina P, 2009. 176.

8. Eric Schmitt. "Compromise on Military Gay Ban Gaining Support among Senators." *New York Times*, 12 May 1993, nytimes.com. Accessed 21 Jan. 2019.

9. Schmitt, "Compromise on Military Gay Ban."

10. Cacilia Kim and Elizabeth Kristen. "Don't Ask Don't Tell Is Still Destroying Lives." *HuffPost*, 20 Sept. 2016, huffingtonpost.com. Accessed 21 Jan. 2019.

SOURCE NOTES CONTINUED

11. Collins et al., *Uniform Discrimination*, 10.

12. "Key Dates in US Military LGBT Policy." *Naval History Blog*, US Naval Institute, 26 Mar. 2018, navalhistory.org. Accessed 21 Jan. 2019.

13. Buzz Bissinger. "Don't Ask, Don't Kill." *Vanity Fair*, May 2005, vanityfair.com. Accessed 21 Jan. 2019.

CHAPTER 6. THE WAR ON TERROR AND REPEAL OF DADT

1. Steve Estes. *Ask and Tell: Gay and Lesbian Veterans Speak Out*. U of North Carolina P, 2009. 233.

2. Nathaniel Frank, *Unfriendly Fire: How the Gay Ban Undermines the Military and Weakens America*. Macmillan, 2009. 209.

3. John Files. "Gay Ex-Officers Say 'Don't Ask' Doesn't Work," *New York Times*, 10 Dec. 2003, nytimes.com. Accessed 21 Jan. 2019.

4. Kyle Swenson. "The Air Force Expelled Her in 1955 for Being a Lesbian. Now, at 90, She's Getting an Honorable Discharge." *Washington Post*, 18 Jan. 2018, washingtonpost.com. Accessed 21 Jan. 2019.

5. Dave Philipps. "Ousted as Gay, Aging Veterans Are Battling Again for Honorable Discharges." *New York Times*, 6 Sept. 2015, nytimes.com. Accessed 21 Jan. 2019.

6. Philipps, "Ousted as Gay."

7. Philipps, "Ousted as Gay."

8. Valerie M. Buck. "Correcting Your Military Discharge." *Senior Veterans Service Alliance*, n.d., veteransaidbenefit.org. Accessed 21 Jan. 2019.

9. Chuck Hadad et al. "Transgender Ex-Navy SEAL Lives in 'Gray World.'" *CNN*, 4 Sept. 2014, cnn.com. Accessed 21 Jan. 2019.

10. Emily Wax-Thibodeaux. "'We All Have the Right to Defend Freedom': Transgender Veterans Speak Out against Trump's Ban." *Washington Post*, 29 Mar. 2018, washingtonpost.com. Accessed 21 Jan. 2019.

CHAPTER 7. LIFE AS AN LGBTQ SOLDIER

1. Brian VanHooker. "I Had to Come Out Five Different Times after Joining the Army." *MEL Magazine*, n.d., melmagazine.com. Accessed 21 Jan. 2019.

2. "What It's Like Being Gay/Bisexual in the Military." *YouTube*, uploaded by Saige Santana, 4 May 2018, youtube.com. Accessed 21 Jan. 2019.

3. "What It's Like Being Gay/Bisexual in the Military."

4. Stephanie Russell-Kraft. "'Don't Ask, Don't Tell' Is Gone, but Its Effects Still Haunt LGBT Veterans." *Task & Purpose*, 28 Feb. 2018, taskandpurpose.com. Accessed 21 Jan. 2019.

5. Nicole Puglise. "'Don't Ask, Don't Tell': Military Members 'Out and Proud' Five Years after Repeal." *Guardian*, 27 Sept. 2016, theguardian.com. Accessed 21 Jan. 2019.

6. Puglise, "'Don't Ask, Don't Tell.'"

7. VanHooker, "I Had to Come Out Five Different Times."

8. Puglise, "'Don't Ask, Don't Tell.'"

9. Erin Faith Wilson. "Women in Uniform: What It's Like to Be a Lesbian in the Military." *After Ellen*, 23 Sept. 2015, afterellen.com. Accessed 21 Jan. 2019.

10. Wilson, "Women in Uniform."

11. Tamar Lewin. "Gay Groups Suggest Marines Selectively Prosecute Women." *New York Times*, 4 Dec. 1988, nytimes.com. Accessed 21 Jan. 2019.

12. Wilson, "Women in Uniform."

13. German Lopez. "Letting LGBTQ Soldiers Serve Isn't Just for Equality. It Also Makes the Military Stronger." *Vox*, 17 Jan. 2017, vox.com. Accessed 21 Jan. 2019.

14. Lopez, "Letting LGBTQ Soldiers Serve."

CHAPTER 8. THE FUTURE OF LGBTQ PEOPLE IN THE MILITARY

1. Heather Marie Stur. "Donald Trump's 'Trans Ban' Reverses More Than 70 Years of Military Integration." *Washington Post*, 29 Jan. 2019, washingtonpost.com. Accessed 31 Jan. 2019.

2. "LGBT Pride Month." *STAND-TO!*, US Army, 8 June 2017, army.mil. Accessed 21 Jan. 2019.

3. Erik Larson. "US Soldiers with HIV Say Trump's New Policy Will Force Them Out." *Bloomberg*, 19 Jul. 2018, bloomberg.com. Accessed 21 Jan. 2019.

4. Sitaji Gurung. "Despite Policy Changes, LGBT Military Personnel Still Experiencing Sexual Trauma and Discrimination." *CUNY Graduate School of Public Health and Health Policy*, 8 Jan. 2018, sph.cuny.edu. Accessed 21 Jan. 2019.

5. Corey Dickstein. "Pentagon: Mattis' 'Deploy or Get Out' Policy Is Working." *Stars and Stripes*, 2 Oct. 2018, stripes.com. Accessed 21 Jan. 2019.

INDEX

ABOUT THE AUTHORS

DUCHESS HARRIS, JD, PHD

Dr. Harris is a professor of American Studies at Macalester College and curator of the Duchess Harris Collection of ABDO books. She is also the coauthor of the titles in the collection, which features popular selections such as *Hidden Human Computers: The Black Women of NASA* and series including News Literacy and Being Female in America.

Before working with ABDO, Dr. Harris authored several other books on the topics of race, culture, and American history. She served as an associate editor for *Litigation News*, the American Bar Association Section of Litigation's quarterly flagship publication, and was the first editor in chief of *Law Raza*, an interactive online journal covering race and the law, published at William Mitchell College of Law. She has earned a PhD in American Studies from the University of Minnesota and a JD from William Mitchell College of Law.

JILL C. WHEELER

Jill C. Wheeler is the author of more than 300 nonfiction titles for young readers. Her interests include biographies and the natural and behavioral sciences. She lives in Minneapolis, Minnesota, where she enjoys sailing, riding motorcycles, and reading.